Real Wealth Revealed

AWAKE

Marilyn J. Macha

Published by Efluential Publishing a division of Efluential Marketing LLC

www.EfluentialPublishing.com

First Printing December 2014

CONTENTS

INTRODUCTION

The primary purpose for writing this book, and simply having words on paper (or on a computer screen) for reference, is to provide easily available access to thoughts and ideas that could alter, in a good way, your relationship with money and the ideas you have about yourself. And, also, to reveal that love is everywhere in the world. All problems in this world come from our thinking—all of them—because we take action out of our thoughts. How we think about ourselves, others, and the world at large determines what we then do, which in turn creates what we have, and what our life looks like as a result.

If it's money that you want—and you're reading this to support having more money—then the good news is that what I'm about to reveal will show you how to have more money. But you'll discover along the way that it's really not about "the money." You also may be surprised at how you actually get "more money."

To begin with, it is my intention to provide you with the clarity of getting just how amazing you really are. I want you to "get" your own greatness—because it's certainly there. It may be hidden just below the layers that life has piled upon you (and what you've thought *about* that), but the diamond of who you really are is just lying below the surface and still waiting to be discovered by the most important person in the world—and that person is YOU!

More Than Material Possessions

Another intention I have is for you to know this, fully and deeply, down to your core: It is not what you have in material possessions, but who you are, that creates "real wealth." The greatest human error is to look at what you have in order to determine *who* you are. That is simply backwards thinking and we will explore that more within this book.

Just for fun, did you know what a Google search for the definition of "wealth" reveals? When looking at how it is presented here, I actually smirked:

Wealth - *welth/*noun

an abundance of valuable possessions or money.

"He used his wealth to bribe officials."

synonyms: *affluence, prosperity, riches, means, substance, fortune; money, cash, lucre, capital, treasure, finance; assets, possessions, resources, funds; property, stock, reserves, securities, holdings;* informal *wherewithal, dough, moolah*

-the state of being rich; material prosperity.

"Some people buy boats and cars to display their wealth."

In going deeper in my investigation, I found the definition that I just knew was available (we really do find what we look for). The word "wealth" is a thirteenth-century Old English word meaning well-being and happiness! Well-being and happiness! That is "real wealth," which, of course, still includes money.

Where's the Love, Where is the Joy

Another big intention of mine, and what I am looking to serve here, is this idea of "Who am I *being* to myself, others, and in the world at large? And, who am I *being* for my clients?" What I would love to do is to marry the left-brain thinking—that side of you that deals with the circumstances in your life—with the right-side of your brain, which is where true happiness and joy can be found.

I want to not only bring joy to the financial industry (the place where I resided for thirty years in professional terms) and in our thinking *about* money, but I'd also like it to be present for just about everyone I run into on a daily basis. One way to access that joy is to be a part of something larger than ourselves. This will help us explore our expansion and our human connection in depth as we progress, with joy!

It's an "Inside-Out" Job

Let's talk about the term "real wealth" for a minute. What exactly does that mean? Well, one thing I know for sure is that it is an "inside-out job." And, that finding inner peace and happiness along your journey toward financial wealth is really what it's all about.

No matter what the present circumstances are, you can generate a life you love living powerfully from within. That is where the real power lies. There are ways to find a sense of well-being and aliveness—and this is where we are going by using the tools presented in this book. Not just that, but we will also find a greater sense of fulfillment, depth, and freedom.

My goal is to help move you from your head to your heart—with your thinking, from your analytical mind to the subconscious. And what I truly want is to bring more joy to the financial industry in particular. This is what gets me up in the morning, and why I can honestly say, "I love my life!" I simply love what I do.

The Arrangement of Time

I also want to illustrate the need to create harmony in our lives, rather than striving to find balance. Balance is an interpretation; harmony is a way of "being" in the world. There is always a dance when it comes to balance, and even if you can't be in two places at the same time, when we are in harmony with all we are attempting to accomplish, we can then create a space that is in alignment with our purpose and goals. This has much to do with the arrangement of time. And this is another area we will dive into more.

In the late 90s I came across some really great advice. As suggested by the author Bill Bachrach, "In the grand scheme of things, money's not that important. It's important only to the extent that it allows you to enjoy what's important to you. And not worrying about your finances is critical to having a life that excites you, nurtures those you love, and fulfills your highest aspirations. You want to make smart choices about money, based on what is important to you—your core values—and build a financial strategy, starting with your own unique values—those things that are truly important to you."

He goes on to say, "By defining these unique values, you can create a plan that not only looks good on paper, but spurs you to follow through and achieve your goals." What he is talking about is creating a value-based financial plan that "will help you realize what's important to you, align your financial choices with the great life you want, and become inspired to do whatever it takes to have that life."

This advice sparked a deep "knowing" inside of me and started my own discoveries of well-being and happiness. In doing so, I found some amazing answers hidden within me, and it is with great pleasure that I share a peek at these valuable insights with you now.

What if this life simply is about the experience of itself? Not the worry, not the doubt, not the fear, but the adventure of discovery? What would those new tools look like, if this life simply is about the experience of itself—for the experience, itself?

Listen deeply: *Ask questions of yourself and listen deeply to the answers. My dear friend Mary Morrissey told me many times that the quality of your life is determined by the quality of questions that you ask. I add further that the more you ask yourself—and of yourself—in the tone of love and curiosity, the richer your life becomes. How could it apply to your own life? What would you have it mean in your own experience of life? How could it develop your own consciousness, your own* *awareness of "being" in the world? Begin to ask these questions as you listen to your inner thoughts.*

Feel life: *the full gamut of emotions. What that means is, be willing to feel fear and take an action step anyway. So often our fears are residue from past experiences of a person whom we are not anymore. Simply be willing. My grandson spent the night and wanted to help me prepare breakfast. He was tentative as he tapped the egg on the side of the bowl, and when I helped him approach the task with more determination, the shell, indeed, did break. As I watched him I saw fear in his eyes as the shell broke and the egg white got onto his fingers. Perhaps some earlier reprimand in his young life brought back a memory of feeling bad, scared, embarrassed to have broken something. He didn't want to break any more eggs! Sometimes when something happens that has an adverse response to what we would want, we allow that interpretation to thwart future actions that are not truly related. We stop our experiences, our adventure of life! Be aware of your interpretation of your feelings. (He is now my "egg breaker" for all recipes, with encouragement and practice!)*

These valuable insights are just a taste of what I would like to share with you in this book. I am thrilled you are here to take this voyage with me. Seeking all the riches of the world is nice—exciting, in fact—but what is inside you is where the real treasures lie.

What is "Real Wealth" to Me?

"Real Wealth" is about tapping into our greatness, and being great in and for the world; to serve and make a difference. James Allen, philosophical writer of the late 1800s and early 1900s, says, "We can't outperform our own self-image." If our lives are to expand, our monetary wealth to grow, we must expand our own thinking, first, about ourselves.

True "Real Wealth" includes all areas of life: health, wealth, love, and purpose. Making millions and millions does not solve our issues, nor does it get you to the real meaning in life. In fact, making or having more money often compounds issues, gives us more to worry about, to manage, to protect. Unless our own image of ourselves is solid, and aligned with our core values, life will be a struggle. When we come from a secure sense of who we really are, to begin with, and then grow our financial affairs, money becomes a tool with which we make a difference in our own lives *and* the lives of others.

The main thing here is to shift our focus from just going out there chasing the money and trying to make more money—into knowing there is more to wealth than money. There is a larger and fuller existence available to us. It's way more about getting engaged in questioning what "my" life is really about; and taking a look at spirituality, purpose, relationships—and again, that there is more to "Real Wealth" than money.

It's like Christmas morning, and looking at all these presents under the tree. There is more available to us; a much fuller and larger existence that ties everything together and is more expansive in nature.

A Grander Life of Purpose

Society has kept us believing that there is a set way to go about your life. Go to school and get a great job. Get married, get the house, and acquire things to make you happy. Society has gotten us to buy into that belief that this is what our life is all about. You go to school and learn. Make some money. Then you die. But there is so much more to life than that. There is the gift of you, and what you are bringing forth is the awareness to a fuller, grander life of purpose.

How I define "Real Wealth" is, in part, the experience of being "awake" and "aware." It is the expansion of knowing who we are and what is possible.

Again, the word "wealth" is a thirteenth-century Middle English word meaning well-being and happiness. "Real Wealth" is the result of having a life you love living. And, when living inside "Real Wealth," you wake up in the morning and say "I love my life!" I have been studying these aspects for over twenty years, and my advisory practice has given me much fodder to develop—and distinguish the thoughts creating my life and the lives of my clients.

Who is Marilyn Macha?

In my own journey toward "Real Wealth," I began to learn that it's more about the wealth inside that matters most. And, in looking at where I began, I was very far off the path of true wealth, indeed. I looked to others to take care of me. I didn't believe in me. And sometimes, I didn't even trust others to take care of me.

Here's a Snapshot of My Life Back Then

I began in the financial services industry in 1982, freshly divorced, replanted from Kansas City to my home in Houston, with my five-year-old son. Having been a housewife for those last five years, I was eager to prove myself in a career. I began selling business insurance in the Property & Casualty field, and received my training there in order to "cold call" executives of companies.

After three years, "financial planning" was getting much attention in the press, and having taken primarily math classes in college, I just knew that I would enjoy the number crunching analysis. Little did I know that the beginning of this career was as much about investing in myself and in others, more than investing in products for clients.

I did not have the depth of understanding of who I was or what I was doing, let alone really be capable of doing. I was making a living, but not living a life. And I used my son as an excuse to build a career. What I know now is, I mistakenly thought I had to spend more time there, building my career, because I didn't really believe, nor trust deeply, that I could take care of us. I was basically running scared and trying to *make* a life for me and my son.

What Happened Next...

I built a successful practice as an investment advisor and had six advisors working with me—with about $500 million in assets under management. I had a good life. I met a wonderful man, John, and we got married. The young man that I relied on for his incredible investment expertise within my business wanted to expand, and I stepped into his dream for the company. And, even though I loved that, I eventually realized it wasn't my dream.

I wondered about this every morning, and worried. I woke up not knowing how I was going to do that day, other than just suit up and show up—and I wasn't happy. My son was recently engaged, and several years later, they had my first grandson. They lived in Kansas City, we lived in Houston, and I wasn't with them very often—although there was a yearning to be.

I didn't know how to transition to a life near my son and his family. It looked like leaving my business, in order to have what I wanted, was all but impossible.

My marriage was good, but most often I picked on my husband. I picked on him because I was annoyed with my own life. So I found little things in his life to be annoyed about. Anybody else do that?

What My Life Looks Like Today

John, my husband, is precious. He is an exceptional man. He supports me with so much love and, as an accomplished musician, gifts me with beautiful music. We own a second home in Kansas City, and I go up there to visit my two grandbabies once a month for at least ten days to two weeks at a time. I sold my practice to the young man whose dream I wanted to support. The company we built together is now his, and I watch him grow in making a difference in the financial world for so many others.

This all came about out of the lessons and structure that I am sharing in this book. I stood in what I would love, separate from what my life looked like at the time, and I saw that the business "we" were running was his passion, and I kept taking "sweet, small steps" with my vision clearly in mind, so that everything worked out for all of us.

I found support. People showed up in my life to support me in both my personal learning and in my business. I asked Einstein's question, "Is the universe friendly?" and if it's friendly, am I supported in that? I came to answer with a resounding "yes."

I have met so many fabulous and loving people that support my vision. Having been in the investment world for thirty years, and by training clients how to have security about their money and not anxiety, is how I learned what "Real Wealth" is—and that money is just a medium in life to have the availability to do whatever you want to do, give whatever you want to give, and be comfortable enough, and to be creative enough to give your true gifts in life.

I teach, and at the time of writing this book, I am blessed to be coaching seven successful investment advisors who have reached their own glass ceilings, how to break through and have a whole life that they love living—and not just a business, which got me to the next step. I am creating a whole training program for entrepreneurs on business with heart.

I am also a Licensed Academy Trainer and certified coach, and that has put me in front of great audiences. I've learned a coaching system that produces real transformation for people. My client list has grown rapidly, and my ability to see me for who I came to be has increased. And, most importantly, I am no longer under the weight of feeling like I have to do something that isn't really mine to do.

In other words, I feel like I am continuing to unleash and unlock myself each and every day—and that's what this work and thinking provides. By my example, you can see this in living color; in the form of one woman who went after her dreams, who took on the task and got support, and then learned a system of transformation to teach in the world.

How This Applies to Life

What if I could provide a glimpse of an expanded view for a well-rounded life—with a roadmap to where true wealth lies? And, let me say right up front, it's not in the dollars and the riches—it's in the quality of your relationships. It's in how deeply you can love. Are you following your purpose? Are you living a life that you love living? Are you healthy enough to enjoy that?

Would an inquiry into these questions improve the quality of your life? I have found that it's more about how your thoughts and perspective on life lead you to the results of living a wealthy life, and living a life you imagined. This includes money, love, career, health, plus how we think and how we show up in any situation life brings our way.

My favorite personal revelation is the fact that it's more important (and actually less burdensome) to look at my own thinking and tell myself the truth about what I really think. What's *under* what I'm thinking about? What's under what my thinking **is** about—and what my thinking **is** about will reveal the tone, the direction, the meaning that only I am giving my life.

Unless they are sick, people typically don't wake up worried about health. Unless they are someone who is going through a divorce, they don't usually wake up worried about being alone. Except for those out of work, most people don't wake up worried about their careers. Mostly, they wake up worried about money and thinking that money will solve their problems.

That is what I'd like to speak to here, that false belief that money, in itself, will make you happy and whole. It's our thinking and what we are telling ourselves about ourselves that determines our results and our sense of security. No amount of money in the world will provide that. That is an internal conversation with the "self!" "Real Wealth" is the "Joy of Life." And it's being happy and having everything that you love.

Building a Solid Foundation

How I define the structure to begin to create a life filled with wealth is with a metaphor of "the four pillars," or cornerstones as I like to call them, that are so foundational to living a life of "Real Wealth," and without having that, we tend to just drift aimlessly along in life.

Without these four pillars, you just go from project to project, relationship to relationship, state to state, house to house, or whatever. Make money, get into debt—make money, get into debt. Get married, get divorced—get married, get divorced. Get the idea?

I am reminded of the purpose behind writing this book. You see, my mother was a great woman. She was well-loved, and such a sweet lady that everyone could not help but fall in love with her. But she didn't think she was great, even though she really was.

This book is for her, Jane Law Macha. She passed away several years ago at the wonderful age of 93, still loving and being loved. She is the inspiration of my desire to teach what I have learned: that we came to share our gifts, all of us, and that each of us can show, like a seedling, with adequate nurturing, love, support and the desire to find out *who we really are*.

We all need to be reminded that our contributions are important in the world. Thinking about this gives me a renewed sense of purpose. It drives me to do my best each and every day (when I am "awake"!) and to let others know that what they do, and who they are, is great—and it matters!

ABOUT THIS BOOK

As noted above, living a life of "Real Wealth" is built upon a foundation of four main components, and in this book we cover the first of those four pillars. What you explore here is "Awake," which is one of the four foundational cornerstones. Keep in mind that each pillar leads us to the next one.

These four foundational pillars, parts, or cornerstones cover everything from **Being Awake** to how I think => which leads to **Being Aware** of how I behave => that turns into **Being Curious** about this behavior => and **Being Willing** to make a change in my thinking and behaviors to create a different outcome or result.

The operative word here is "being": living to your true potential in four main areas of your life—health, wealth, relationships, and purpose. So, let's take a quick look to get a general idea of what is to come, and what each of these four pillars is all about:

Awake

The first step, and perhaps the most obvious step, is to be AWAKE; wake up to your thinking. Without this nothing great can be consciously created. Being awake is to know when we are constricted. It is where we are to begin our journey toward living a life we love.

Aware

Once you are awake, it's easy to start noticing thought patterns. And now you are at least awake enough to become AWARE of your thoughts. Being aware gives you greater structure to fulfill all of your desires, and to know that all is possible.

Curious

When we talk about getting CURIOUS, it is really all about asking ourselves questions, looking inside—not outside in the world. Then by being introspective and truthful with ourselves, we find ourselves being even more curious about life's deeper truths.

Willing

The final part is where we become WILLING to make the changes necessary in both our thinking and behaviors to create a different result or outcome. We begin to take action where we have stopped before. We are willing to do what it takes!

When we incorporate all four cornerstones into our daily lives, we can then embrace our journey toward a life of true "Real Wealth." So, let's get started!

AWAKE

Being "Awake" to "what my thinking is about" has been avoided by the majority of people across the globe. How do I know this? Look at what we continue to create: distrust, war, competition, disrespect, hatred, and pillaging our natural resources. The bottom line is many of us are no longer content with this way of thinking (or NOT thinking).

As a skill, being "Awake" is paramount in our self-discovery, in our interpretations, our perceptions, our abilities to take on new ideas and growth; it is absolutely required to build a business, to be in a caring relationship, or to make a difference in the world. Without it our lives and our self-esteem are all based in what has already happened, and all from a default paradigm from the past. As you begin to read this part, do so as if you *were not* already "Awake," and that you are waking up. It will make a difference to begin with an inquisitive mind.

CHAPTER 1
INTUITION

In This Chapter

*   Listening to that still, soft voice instead of all the noise in your head

*   Using intuition as a personal navigation system to guide your path

*   Finding ways to elevate your thoughts and to trust your internal voice

"There may be 7 billion plus brains in the world, but there is only one mind, and you are a personal expression of that one mind."

– Bob Proctor, philosopher featured in The Secret

Being "Awake" is the premise in which we can distinguish and experience—both consciously and deliberately—our intuition. It means that I'm not alone and it's not just me coming up with ideas and answers. Paradoxically, knowing that I am a part of something larger than my own thinking is comforting to me, and that I can awaken to, listen to, and trust ideas and thoughts that come to me. These are new ideas, and not just ideas from the past, from my brain, from already laid down synaptic paths (which are derived from past experiences and conclusions that I made).

In this combined study of psychology, neuroscience, and quantum physics, I discovered that everything is energy. This includes everything in the universe. What is also interesting is that there is an energy field and a voice of wisdom within this energy field—both of which I am a part. And when my mind gets quiet, I can actually hear this.

However, I must be "Awake" to hear this voice. It is when I can be still to listen—and be awake to a voice of wisdom speaking to me in my thoughts—that I get to experience being a part of something bigger than just myself. After all, if it's "me" speaking to "me," why would it occur as another voice guiding me?

The difference between knowing if it's the "voice of wisdom" or just "my human voice" (noise) is that the latter is about doubt, confusion, and worry. The voice of wisdom is nurturing and forwarding and expansive in nature. The noise is limiting and worrisome.

---

in·tu·i·tion int(y)o͞o'iSH(ə) n/ noun

the ability to understand something immediately, without the need for conscious reasoning.

"We shall allow our intuition to guide us."

synonyms: instinct, intuitiveness; sixth sense, clairvoyance, second sight

a thought that one knows or considers likely from instinctive feeling rather than conscious reasoning.

"Your insights and intuitions as a native speaker are positively sought."

synonyms: hunch, feeling (in one's bones), inkling, (sneaking) suspicion, idea, sense, notion

---

So, what does intuition mean to me? Most importantly, it means that I'm not alone, and it's not just me coming up with all the answers. I have come to know there is an energy field, and there is also a voice of wisdom within that energy field. Both of which are things I am a part of, and when my mind gets quiet, as noted, the great thing is that I can hear it.

An All-Knowing "Essence" Speaks to Me

Again, the first aspect of intuition is knowing I am not alone. But it's even more than that. It's also knowing I am not my personality. I am not my body. I am not my mind. I have a personality. I have a body. I have a mind. And I am so much *more* by being a part of this energy field. I have support, power, and a strength that comes to me through my intuition. When I really begin to rely and trust in this power, I receive answers that are, quite simply, profound in nature. It's as if an "all-knowing essence" is speaking directly to me, or through me, by way of my thoughts.

The gift of intuition also supports me with a guidance I can either adhere to, or not. It's my choice. And with that choice comes the consequence of our actions. For example, assume I have a thought of "bring your umbrella to the office today," and then discount that idea as unnecessary—since it's a beautiful day with blue skies overhead. Now really, why would I want to bother taking my umbrella?

Well, perhaps I didn't know a storm was brewing off in the distance, and that it would be helpful and useful for me to have that umbrella later on that afternoon. If I had known, certainly I would have brought it in order to have an umbrella when I came out of the office after work. Who in their right mind wouldn't? Otherwise, I'd get drenched in the sudden downpour of rain.

This simple illustration above validates intuition, and the useful guidance it can provide. If I had followed this intuition, and acted upon it, I would have been better prepared for what had not been on my personal radar when I left the house earlier that morning.

That is one of the many ways that intuition can serve us in a positive way within our lives.

The Voice of Inspired Insight

How do I tell the difference between the voice of my intuition and the voice of my ego, or fear, or any other voice that I may have? I truly love how my mentor and friend, Mary Morrissey, describes this: "Imagine the phone rings and you pick it up and it is someone you know and love very well. It may be a spouse or one of your children, or perhaps one of your friends, and they go 'hi' and call you by name. You know that voice. You recognize that voice. How do you know that voice from all of the other voices who may call you from time to time, such as telemarketers, for example?"

Mary continues with, "You know them, and the voice, that frequency, because you got interested in them, you have a relationship with them, you invested in a relationship and over time you came to know their voice among all other voices. And it's exactly the same with the voice of inspired insight, the voice that comes from the intelligence of the universe that is operating right at the center of your own being. You can know unmistakably. You feel it as a hunch, you sense it as guidance, you know it as that brilliant idea that comes to you. It is inspired insight."

You see, when we are "Awake," or you begin to awaken, our intuition is one of the first faculties that presents itself. When we wake up, we are then capable of hearing that "still, soft voice" that can't be analyzed or proven in the physical world. It is a part of the energy field which is always speaking to us, guiding us, and never explaining or reasoning with us; simply an idea, a thought, a knowing, a "wow, what a great idea" knowing.

Begin to listen newly; when you do you will also know that you are awakening. Gandhi called it "the voice of truth" and I add that it is always calm, graceful, and clear. It is as loud as the commitment to being "Awake." But what we *do* with the thoughts and ideas that come to us through our intuition is a completely different topic.

A Stream of Flowing Water

Intuition is a constant stream of ideas and thoughts, intelligent, loving, and resourceful, guiding us toward to life we would love living; a life we came to share, to know, and to experience. Our intuition is always speaking to us. The role we play with intuition is how "Awake" am I to be able to hear its voice. And, therefore, how "Awake" am I committed to *being,* in order to experience life newly, profoundly, joyously?

This is truly a life worth living, and the life possible in becoming fully "Awake." Our own intuition is always there, and in all ways, speaking to us. Am I listening? Am I awake enough to even know this voice exists?

And if I have experienced the phenomenon of intuition before, am I committed to waking up even more vibrantly, thus opening up my capacity to hear even more from this "voice of truth," this "voice of inspired insight"? If we do, we will experience a world of love and compassion, and ourselves as *being* passionate and joyous. This is what is possible—it is what you will discover with your newfound capacity to hear your intuition speaking to you.

Your Personal GPS System

Bob Proctor, who was featured on the phenomenal DVD called *The Secret,* describes it as this: "I have a highly evolved intuitive factor. I wasn't born with it like this. I was raised much like everybody else and thought this was a bunch of nonsense. However, I gained a better understanding of this years ago, and it is something I became fascinated with and worked at developing it. How do you develop it? You pay attention to it."

If you get on the frequency of intuition, you can pick up the higher-level thoughts that many of the worlds great minds have tapped into. Einstein, Henry Ford, Benjamin Franklin, many of these great thinkers knew how to tap into the brilliance of their intuition and higher intelligence. They were no different from you and me, they simply perfected the use of this mental faculty often enough that it became a trusted habit.

Here's another thought about intuition. You may have experienced a time when a friend and you were talking about someone in common, and at the same time your friend either gets a phone call or text from that very same person you were talking about. He may have replied, "Your ears must have been burning, because we were just talking about you!" Coincidence? I think not. It's more a matter of tapping into that higher frequency and vibration of thought.

Everyone resides in this same energy field. Successful people are simply more "Awake" than others (in the areas where they focus their desire for success), and have learned, through repetition and validating results, to pay attention to their intuition. These individuals are "Awake" more often than they are asleep—awake to their thoughts, their actions, their clear decisions, and their listening capacity to their intuitive voice.

So, let's take the earlier example a step further. Do you suppose that person called because you were talking about them? Or, perhaps the reason you were actually talking about them was because that person was thinking about your friend? Either way, it doesn't really matter. It makes no difference. What matters is that there is a frequency and energy that we can tap into that reveals more than meets the physical eye.

And, if we get interested in this, pay attention to this, and practice using our intuition faculties, it can be a reliable source of information and guidance. As Mary so eloquently put this, it can become your trusted "voice of inspired insight."

Looking At Our Thoughts

Empower VS. Disempower

"You are going to have to lose your mind and create a new one."

– Dr. Joe Dispenza,

Now that we see just how powerful our intuition can be—and the thoughts and ideas which guide us in an easier, clearer, less stressful direction—we must recognize that along with this comes the responsibility for choosing our thoughts wisely. It is here where we experience the skill of being "Awake" in order first, to see what our thoughts are, and then, secondly, to be able to guide them ourselves.

The fact remains, little do most people realize just how much control we actually have over the circumstances within our lives. It's really not the circumstances that we can control, but our relationship *to* them and our reaction or response related to the circumstances We absolutely do have control over all of these, for example: what I choose to think; the direction in which I am willing to take my life; what I am more interested in; wherever I put my attention, I will get more of; am I more interested in holding a resentment, or am I more interested in being a loving spouse. This all takes practice, and it takes being "Awake" to what I am thinking!

We commonly hear "what we focus on expands," and "like attracts like," "we must be diligent as to what we allow into our minds." As such, I know I can only control my thoughts *about* something, and in choosing a thought that would empower me, or the situation, and will create a different result.

Let's take a look at how we were trained in life, as in polar opposites. We're trained beginning in the crib that things and actions are labeled "good-bad, right-wrong, should-shouldn't, can-can't." Life becomes what other people tell us "life is about"; and then we get labeled as a rebel or a conformist, depending on what point of view we take as our own. It's all about judgments, survival.

There are many things we have decided about ourselves, and about others, that aren't even the truth, but we live as though what we think is true IS true. We make our own meaning about life from our thinking. But our true power lies just underneath, as in "what am I thinking?" This is where the real power is, because it's our thinking that creates our results.

For example, I knew a woman who said that she really wanted a loving man in her life, and she affirmed "I am in a loving relationship..." over and over again. But every evening when she came home, she parked her one car in the middle of her two-car garage, and daily she thought about where *she* would go over the holidays by herself. Her thoughts and her actions were not in alignment with her affirmation. She had to become "Awake" to how, and what, she was thinking and what her actions were emphasizing.

So, right now, what am I thinking? Being "Awake," being "Aware"... ahhh, do you see how this all connects? And then when we get "Curious" about this, and there's a conscious choice to be "Willing" to do the right thing and to be more "right" (in the sense of what is the action that is aligned with what you would really love and aligned with what's really important to you), that's where we connect the dots.

Everything Has a Certain Vibration to It

Again, we must be cognizant as to what types of thoughts we are thinking. Do we tend to choose to think positive and uplifting thoughts? Or are we defaulting to more negative and downward spiraling thoughts? It's time to wake up to what my thoughts are and consequently what those thoughts are bringing to me.

According to quantum physics, everything is energy, meaning that everything has a vibration; the slower and heavier something is in the physical world, the denser its vibration—the slower and more immovable its space is. So, is it that our thoughts are also energy and have their own vibration? And if our thoughts are disempowering, might it not make sense that they would be very dense and lethargic?

That's why, when we get on a downward cycle of negative thinking, it takes much more energy to move away from that space. It's better simply to identify if my thoughts are empowering or disempowering to begin with, to be "Awake" to having them, and choose newly. Empowering thoughts more resemble the energy and vibration of our dreams. They are aligned with our vision, and are lighter and less dense.

Think about it—when you feel great, when you're happy, when you're thrilled with anticipation—the energy is electric *and* light. When you're depressed, feeling guilty, or ashamed, how heavy do you feel? Very, I would suspect. Be more interested in holding empowering thoughts, and watch your life magnify, and attract the positive into your life.

Perhaps Losing One's Mind is Good

Dr. Joe Dispenza is an expert on change, the brain, and mind and human potential. He is the author of *Evolve Your Brain: The Science of Changing Your Mind*, a neuroscientist, chiropractor, lecturer, and was featured in the movie *What the Bleep Do We Know!?* And, as such, Dr. Dispenza has some interesting points to note are far as our thinking patterns go.

He says, "When we fully lay down the old, familiar life, or mind, and start creating the new, there is a moment between the two worlds that is bereft of anything we know, and most rush back from this void to the familiar. That place of uncertainty—the unknown—is what the maverick, the mystic, and the saint know to be fertile ground." Familiar is not necessarily good, it just means that is what your mind is more comfortable doing. There is a part of the brain called the amygdala. It's the part of the brain that helps our species survive, but its primary purpose is to look for danger, and to look for what could go wrong.

There are tools and skills to allow this, and we will get into this more later on, but for now, just know that sometimes we need to "lose our mind" and opt for using our intuitions and higher council instead.

Our Thoughts Matter

Dr. Dispenza also goes on to say, "Your attention is where your energy is. Put all of your attention on the external, material world, and that becomes your investment in reality. On the contrary, command your mindfulness to unfold a deeper aspect of yourself, and your energy will expand that reality…"

Energy goes where your attention flows. Why is this important? Because if we want to transform our reality to create a life we truly love living—have relationships that we dream of, have all the money we desire in order to do the things we want to do, give with a generous heart all the gifts and contributions that inspire us—we must become "Awake" to the fact that our thoughts matter. Literally, they matter in how our lives are materializing in the physical world.

If I look into my physical reality and I don't like what I see, then it's up to me to become "Awake" to my thinking first, and not try to change the conditions that appear to be present. This doesn't mean I'm not going to take different action steps to alter my physical reality; it means I'm going to look at my thinking first about how the physical world is showing up around me and how my actions come from my thinking. I am the only one, for me, that has the ability and the authority to choose a different thought; a different way of thinking about something.

As I began to transition into my consulting business, I watched myself *not* take the simple action steps necessary to build a successful business (like schedule speaking presentations, make phone appointments with coaching prospects, schedule time to write teaching programs). What I discovered (being committed to being "Awake") is that deep down I had the thought, "It took you twenty years to become a very successful business owner in the investment advisory business; it'll take you just as long to really be successful in this new business." My actions were in alignment with that thought. Once I saw that and became "Awake" to it, I began to take different, more powerful action steps that were aligned with the vision of my new business, and not what my "noise" was telling me.

What I Think Matters

Our entire study in this section is to become "Awake" to the fact that I am *always* thinking something. But *what* am I thinking? Are my thoughts forwarding me toward a vision, a goal—or are they trying to "keep me safe"? Are they empowering to me toward more useful situations, or will my thinking thwart any advancement for me or others? Am I being a beneficial presence—my thoughts will determine that—will my thoughts give rise to my next action step (and taking no action *is* an action step)? What's important to me? What am I willing to do to be aligned with what's important, meaningful, to me? What am I thinking? Not, "What am I thinking about," but "What *is* my thinking about?"

Only I can put the emphasis of my thoughts into the physical world. Most people, in fact, are encouraged to believe something like, "If I could only change what's happening, only change that person, only change how 'they' are thinking, acting, being, *then* I'd be just fine." Well, that's backwards. We must begin by becoming "Awake" to the fact (the scientific fact) that what I think matters—literally—what I think supports and creates my physical reality. This is good news, because the *only thing* I actually have any real control over is my own thinking, my own actions, my own results. I can change my thought. Only I have the power, the control, to change my thought. No one can do that for or to me; only I can.

Instant Gratification and Materialism

Joe Dispenza adds, "If you stop believing that thought is real, you will fall back into materialism and stop doing the work. You'll simply choose some emotional addiction or habit for immediate gratification and then talk yourself out of the possibility." Here is where self-defeating behaviors come in. Now, that most certainly sounds less empowering, does it not?

And I completely agree with his assessment that "Herein lies the dilemma: The future reality we create in our minds does not yet provide sensory feedback, and by the quantum model, our senses should be the last to experience what we create. For this reason, many of us make materialism our law once again, and we go unconscious." We want to feel a certain way—we are addicted to feeling good. If we don't feel good then we think that there's "something wrong."

The skill is to learn to put emotions into our visions that we would love *before* they become material. This will support us to stay out of disappointment (that it's not happening fast enough, for example) and stay out of the thought of giving up or self-sabotage. Again this is what I am speaking to in this entire section. We must become "Awake" to how our mind really works and how we can use it to our advantage (or not).

Really, it all begins with being "Awake" and using our mental faculties, such as intuition, to create a new and better reality for our lives. A life of our own choosing and by design, rather than by default. In other words, defaulting to being asleep or running on old, out-of-date, "no thinking involved" auto-programming.

All material things were once a thought: the chair you're sitting on was a thought first; the clothes you're wearing; the book you're reading. By taking this obvious thought process into the context of being "Awake," then naturally, all material things can be brought into existence from our thinking.

Why is that important? Well, if you have a vision or dream from which you establish goals (all of which reside more in the next pillar of "Aware," so more about that later), then just know there are skills and tools to develop and assist in making those thoughts of your vision, into a *physical* reality.

In the meantime, the purpose of why that is in this section of being "Awake" is because it's important to know that we are laying the foundation for attaining the reality of that vision, from, and ultimately through, our thinking. Enough for now; just be sure to make it a habit to become "Awake" to your thinking, because it truly *is* creating your reality.

Is My Thinking Empowering or Disempowering?

As stated before, and as a cornerstone for our new and empowered life, we must be completely "Awake" to what thoughts we entertain on a regular basis. We simply need to switch channels from disempowering frequencies and tune into those that are life giving and generative. When we do this, we will be well on our way to creating a life we love living.

I grew up in a family where my mother was the submissive one, and my father was dominant and verbally abusive. In my romantic relationships I was either submissive *or* dominant and curt. But, early on, I had decided (my brain/amygdala had programmed it in) that it was less dangerous to be the dominant and threatening one, rather than submissive in order to be safe within a relationship. These relationships didn't go so well, and I didn't have the experience of love and partnership that I had written in a vision—and truly desired for my primary relationships to look like.

I had to become "Awake" to what my thinking was about, and how it told me that I could be "safe." I still awaken to when I automatically go in that direction, but I now have access to a loving, wonderful, supportive relationship that was, well, just not available to me prior to being "Awake."

How Can I Use My Intuition to an Advantage in Business?

In business and in life, these principles work. It makes no matter if we are applying them in preparation of an upcoming meeting, or to our personal relationships. I suggest you use these mental practices on a daily basis to enhance every area of your life; health, wealth, career, and in your relationships with friends, family, and others. It will certainly make a difference.

Trusting Your Heart

Reacting in Judgment, or With Love

"When we are no longer able to change a situation—we are cchallenged to change ourselves."

– Viktor E. Frankl, Austrian Psychologist

Dr. Viktor Frankl, a prolific author who wrote a widely read account of his experiences in the Nazi death camp during World War II, is a perfect example of how to trust your heart, and heed to the intuitions spoken to your own mind. His story of being able to retain his human dignity, even while being prisoner in a horrible concentration camp, is so inspiring.

In particular, let me share a powerful passage from his book *Man's Search for Meaning*: "In spite of all the enforced physical and mental primitiveness of the life in a concentration camp, it was possible for spiritual life to deepen." You see, even though his wife and children had been taken away to be killed, he chose to see something possible through tragedy.

"My mind still clung to the image of my wife. A thought crossed my mind: I didn't even know if she were still alive. I knew only one thing—which I have learned well by now: Love goes very far beyond the physical person of the beloved. It finds its deepest meaning in his spiritual being, his inner self. Whether or not he is actually present, whether or not he is still alive at all, ceases somehow to be of importance."

He wrote of the experiences and understandings he gleaned during captivity, and kept a manuscript of his teachings hidden in his mattress. But once the guards discovered this, they burned those right in front of him, along with his wedding band.

As he felt himself tighten up and braced himself for yet another horror that was his current reality, he realized he could choose his thoughts. It was the only thing they had no control over. And in choosing his thoughts, he said, "You can't make me hate you." He chose love over fear, and he chose to trust from his heart.

Of that he said in particular, "Everything can be taken from a man but one thing: the last of the human freedoms—to choose one's attitude in any given set of circumstances, to choose one's own way." He was basically saying that "the one thing you can't take away from me is the way I choose to respond to what you do to me".

What does it take to have a light heart full of love? It takes a belief in yourself—without that, it most likely won't happen. But most importantly, you must live in gratitude. Because, in gratitude, a heart becomes full.

Be sure to trust in the invisible, and be willing to take the action steps necessary that'll move you toward your dreams. Fear and faith have much in common. They both direct and address something that hasn't happened yet. Which direction will you take your dream? In becoming "Awake," you have a choice in the matter. Intuition speaks to us when we choose trust and faith in life. If your intuition tells you to take an umbrella, then, what the heck, be sure to grab one before you walk out the front door!

Typically, we are trained to react rather than respond. And quite often, when we do react, we do so in fear or judgment. We must always remember this; the only thing we have complete control over is our thoughts, and the only way we have control over them is if we are "Awake" to them. Once you are, you will find that your responses are kinder, softer, and more in integrity with who you really are.

The Wealth Maven's Review:

The moment a baby is born, that baby has the beginnings of becoming "Awake." The metaphor is, literally, waking up into a world of endless, marvelous possibilities. Being "Awake" is an active decision. Babies are not yet awake to the ways of the physical world. The family and people with whom they will interact will assist them, but as babies, they are not yet awake to any choices they will have.

It's not that they don't know *about* these things in physical reality; they don't know that they *exist*. It is in becoming "Awake" to the existence of such phenomena that begins our journey into discovery of who we are, what we can have, and how we will contribute.

As the baby awakens, that child learns that fire is hot and it can burn the skin; they are not aware of any consequences, but they first become "Awake" to the existence of the relationship between a "physical body" and "fire" and "pain." In fact, our overall health relies on being "Awake" to the interactions of our physical realities, and of the relationship between the world and our own bodies.

The first start of a healthy existence is always to know there is an interactive relationship between my body and what I put into it. This is to become "Awake" to the knowing that what I ingest, breathe in, etc., will have an impact, a reaction in my body; whether its consequence will be enhancing or depleting is then to my being "Aware." Primarily, we must always wake up to "it matters what I allow into my body."

But this is only one aspect of becoming "Awake" in our world—and in our thinking. Even more important is what I will "allow into my thinking" and how "Awake" you are *being* right now.

CHAPTER 2
IMAGINATION

In This Chapter

* Diving into the realms of our imaginative mind
* Choosing generative thoughts of empowerment instead of chaos
* Turning up the juice for an expansive life

"Imagination is more important than knowledge."

– Albert Einstein

Each of us is given special gifts at birth. Just like we are given five senses (sight, hearing, taste, touch, and smell) with which to navigate the physical world, we are also gifted with internal gifts that actually create and support how we live in the world. They are the gifts of intuition, imagination, perception, memory, reason, and will. The first three support our understanding and ability of becoming "Awake." Each one of us is born with these abilities, called our mental faculties. Intuition was the one that we looked at in Chapter 1, and next we'll look at our gift of imagination.

Now, in terms of looking specifically at imagination, as kids, we most likely were better at using this gift than we are now. Think back to kindergarten or early grade school, and how many of us had grand dreams of being a fireman or superhero. Or perhaps you planned on being a ballerina or movie star. We had such vivid imaginations and used them frequently.

Fast-forward to our adult lives, and we'll most likely see we are using imagination in a very different way. I'll bet you'll see more of us imagining what we don't want to have happen, rather that imagining what we'd love to have, do, and be. Rather than having vivid and bright imaginations that take us to new and exciting places, we have allowed this gift to be dialed down or used in ways that terrorize us instead of energizing us.

imag· i· na· tion i-,ma-j-ʻna-shā n/ noun

the ability to imagine things that are not real; the ability to form a picture in your mind of something that you have not seen or experienced.

"You can find a solution if you use a little imagination."

synonyms: *creativity, fancy, fantasy; brainstorming, invention, resourcefulness*

the act or power of forming a mental image of something not present to the senses or never before wholly perceived in reality.

"Is it just my imagination, or did the back door just open?"

synonyms: *Inspiration, daydream, delusion, dream; illusion, mind's eye, mirage, pipe dream*

Every single one of us uses pictures or images in our minds, as this is how we really create our world. We literally think in pictures. I really love how this was explained to me one time by Bob Proctor. He said it like this: "When we think of a feather, we don't see the letters f-e-a-t-h-e-r, we have an image of a feather. Why do we do this? Well, there is a science behind this. When we say the word *feather*, we activate our vocal cords by speaking. These vocal cords set up a vibration, which is also known as speech or language, and it vibrates in a way that our ears pick up on. This light message, or vibration, goes flying down a nerve passageway and strikes a group of cells in your brain. The cells that this activates have been impregnated with an image of a feather. So when I say feather I can simultaneously see it in my mind."

The beauty of this is there is a science behind it. Even with a thing such as imagination, or intuition, we can be comforted to know that it's all backed by scientific truth. And knowing this, we can just begin to see just how powerful our mind is and how it can be used for our advantage in life.

As James Allen, a well-known British author, wrote, "All that a man achieves and all that he fails to achieve is the direct result of his own thoughts."

In the last 100 years, science has been able to prove what the great minds of the 1800s and early 1900s era began to discover. We now know that there are more than three dimensions, sub-atomic particles have been seen, and the invisible world is visible now in the world of science. We know that our thoughts have energy, and that they cause particles to move in the invisible world. The mind-body connection is now studied at all the great universities. Neuroscience calculates and programs thought waves. Thoughts are energy—and now science can prove it.

Thoughts Have Energy

Psychology has gained deep knowledge of the human psyche. Scientists can prove how things materialize from thought patterns and energy. All of this is great news, and now validates what the great thinkers of our yesteryears have been saying all along.

Our thinking creates our results. If you are skeptical, please just take it on as a possibility for now. Play with this for a while and see what happens within your own life. Let's see how we can literally cause harmony in our thinking to materialize it in our outer world—and create a life we would love living. Would that be of interest to you? Would that be okay with you? Again, our thinking creates our results—no kidding!

Thomas Edison was an amazing thinker; he spent time every day just in quiet introspection of his thoughts. He would not have done this if it wasn't effective. If it worked for him, I guarantee it will work for you.

Your Creative Mindset

So, let's begin and give it a go, shall we? Start with an image of what you would love your life to be. What would that look like for you? What would you love to create? Just know that since your mind has been programmed to think *from* the conditions of your life, and from what's already in existence, it'll be tempted to revert to that. You'll think, "What can I do with only a couple of hundred dollars per month," or whatever the condition already is.

Instead, start observing this mental activity. When you begin to look at what you would love to have in your life and how you would love to be, at first what you will see is what's automatically there (and why you can't have what you want); until you practice enough, this is what is necessary—and we will build on this foundation in the chapters to follow.

Now you might get the idea that this sort of imagining will only make you feel worse, because you believe given where you are now, what you would love could look pretty impossible. But, just for a moment, what if you could? If you didn't believe it was impossible, what would you do?

Do What You Can with What You Have

Stay in that question, and keep asking, "What could you do now?" So, let's say you wanted a brand new car. What would you do if this wasn't impossible? Or better said, "What could you do if it was possible?" You'd probably go out to visit showroom of the car you wanted to buy. Okay, act on that hunch and do what you can with what you have.

Remember, it doesn't cost a dime to test drive a car; they let you do this for free. But then, I guess you could argue that this again will only make you feel worse, because now you have found the car of your dreams and it costs way more than you could afford to buy. But what if you could?

Don't feel bad if your mind continues to argue for what you can't do, just stay in the question of what you can do (this is normal). That is when the ideas will come to you. Ideas that are in harmony with your desire begin to show up, as if right out of thin air.

For example, what if while you were on the new car lot, you noticed a used car that looked just as good as what you wanted originally; and it was less than half the cost of a new car? What if that was an affordable option for you? If you hadn't gone ahead and visited the dealership while knowing full well you could not afford that new car, you would never have seen the other option. That would be a missed opportunity.

Now you know you are tapping into the frequency of your desires. This is where the larger and more generative ideas reside. This is where great minds like Edison and Einstein and other successful creators of the past found their own solutions. They allowed themselves to stay in the energy of what they wanted to create—and stayed with the question of what they could do with what they had—a bit longer than most of us are willing to do.

Thinking Differently

Choosing Generative Ideas

"Today expect something good to happen to you no matter what occurred yesterday. Realize the past no longer holds you captive. Let the past go. A simply abundant world awaits you."

–Sarah Ban Breathnach, author and publisher

Let's experiment here for a minute. Let's look at how transformation occurs by expanding our awareness and our consciousness. We build our capacity to remember that our "potential" is truly unlimited. This capacity is what we are learning to transform—to learn to love ourselves in a way that IS transformational—not only for our own life, but for lives that we touch. When we transform, our relationships transform.

Our capacity to transform circumstances, or be stuck, stymied, or overwhelmed by these circumstances, has to do with consciousness. My own capacity equals my consciousness—and my consciousness equals my own capacity. So, let's turn up that light on that right now. Let's experiment by turning up our consciousness.

In terms of transformation, there are certain ways of thinking to consider when deeply connecting with our consciousness—and our capacity to become the person that has the life that we would absolutely love living. A very important thing to note is, it is our "thinking" from the inside out that allows Life to show up—not changing things outside so that we are different.

A Truth Greater Than Facts, or Circumstances

Let's begin with the notion that everything is created twice—first as a thought, and then as a thing. And the underlying consciousness, our deep inner thinking, our discovering and revealing, our subconscious thinking, are all vital keys to transformation.

Remember, transformation requires that we begin to "think" differently. It was Einstein who said that "we can't solve our problems at the same level of thinking that we created them." And I believe that.

One way of thinking differently is knowing that transformation requires a consciousness, or mindset, of abundance. What does that mean? If we are in a "struggle mindset" where life is difficult, hard, a game of chance in which we have no say in the matter, then that *is* how life will show up. The world in terms of our physical reality will be reflected back to us, individually, from how we expect it to show up.

Do you want to know what you are thinking? Just look at the results in your life. How are they showing up? *That* is your thinking. So, if you step into a commitment of life showing up newly—with people and things and situations, newly—your thoughts must be of a different energy, and a different vibration. What we think about matters. Most importantly, it's how we think about it, and how we hold our own self-image. A wonderful idea indeed is to have a consciousness or mindset of abundance/wealth—for the joy of life itself, in experiencing a capacity for being filled up with joy and love, and in creativity and sharing that creativity—that continues to provide a deeper and stronger sense of abundance for me.

What I've come to realize, through study, research, and curiosity, in the way life works in the law of consciousness, and in the law of vibration/frequency is that if you have a consciousness of abundance, you just keep attracting more and more of your good to you. When you choose to get more interested in what is possible, rather than why it won't work, you begin to open the door to abundance; you open the door in that part of your mind where "more" is possible than what currently exists in your physical reality.

Transformation is a Way of Thinking Newly

And anytime you consider "the more," you begin to think into abundance. The more often you choose to consider what it is that you love, more than why you can't have it, you start the flow of having a more expanded life. Simple? Yes, and easier said than done. But you're becoming "Awake" to "the more" that is available to you... to us all.

If you don't have a consciousness of abundance, then no matter what you get, it becomes elusive or temporary. It's why "the rich get richer, and the poor get poorer." This is a way of thinking—about how the world works and what's possible. And in order to alter our thinking, the first tool is to look where you think "abundantly" or not. Transformation requires a consciousness of abundance!

Five thousand years ago, in India, there were writings called the Upanishads out of the Sanskrit, which is some of the most ancient teaching on the planet. It says it this way: "From abundance was scooped abundance and more abundance remains," meaning that you cannot overtake your good. You cannot deplete what is possible. There is always more good available.

That's an important thing to remember in terms of personal transformation. This doesn't mean to come from self-centeredness. In the three-dimensional world, you could certainly steal something from someone, to "have" it, but that isn't your good. Your real good is in your consciousness, as in expanding the awareness of who you are, and with that comes an awareness of your possibilities. In other words, your "Real Wealth."

With that comes an awareness that right at the center of your own being, my own being, is the source to turn to, and from which generates ideas, images, and a flow of understanding that gives rise to our choices and decisions—using your imagination for your good and the good of others—followed by actions that produce in form the transformation we are desiring.

Scientific in Nature and Experience

Most of us have heard the saying "Be transformed by the renewing of your mind." But, if you really want to have a transformed life, you must think differently. You can't expect transformation, and for it to be solid or stable, in a mind that is operating from old thinking. So, we can say things like, "I want to transform my love life," or "I want to transform my economic life," or "I want to transform my creative life," but, unless we think differently, nothing will change.

And first, you must be "Awake" to having certain thoughts and "Awake" to the fact that our thoughts create our experiences—our reality. Let me give you an example from my own life:

Remember, this is scientific. We will need to begin using a different frequency in our thoughts; a different vibration, and a deeper knowing or feeling. If we don't, then even when we begin to attract something that looks like what we want, we will not be able to stabilize it. We won't keep it in our field of experience because we are out of harmony with it.

My desire for you is not that you just know about this, but that you apply it to some real concrete aspect of your life—and you begin to see what happens when you work with your consciousness in regard to a circumstance. So, as an experiment, I want you to now imagine some aspect of your life that you would like to transform. Find this area of your life by either a distinct longing or a discontent (or both).

You will either "long" for it to be different, or you'll feel discontent over the way it is—even if you don't yet know what you would like to be different. You don't have to take on your entire life right now, just pick something new you would like to experience, and let's explore ways of living from that frequency.

Our Brain is an Instrument of the Mind

All of us have a connection to an "infinite energy," an "infinite knowing," speaking to us through these gifts of intuition and imagination. In the physical world, through our physical body, our brain is the instrument, much like a radio. Our brain is the instrument of the mind. Just like the radio in your car is not the music—it's an instrument of the music—your brain, my brain, is an instrument of the mind.

Now, since the mind works in images, focus on the possibilities and choose an image that represents that which you seek; choose something that is meaningful to you. And, rather than an image of lack, limitation, or problems, choose an image that gives you life.

An important thing to note is that once you have an image or an idea in mind, there will be a gap between your idea and the form of that idea. Maria Nemeth, founder of the Academy for Coaching Excellence and author the best seller *The Energy of Money,* calls this "trouble at the border." It's as if there is an invisible boundary between what you imagine in your mind, and what you imagine being produced in physical reality.

It was Dr. Maria Nemeth who gave me this image: Picture a blank piece of paper with a horizontal line in the middle of it. The part below we'll call "Visionary Reality" and the space above will be called "Physical Reality." When you are about to take what you imagine into the space of physical reality, you're at "the border"—that gap between visionary reality and physical reality.

Always be "Awake" to those voices of limitation, and then choose newly. Be clear on what it is that you *do* desire—clarity of the vision of what you would love is vital and it takes practice. We must be grounded in our desire rather than in our fears, otherwise the limiting thoughts will win.

When we are "Awake" to what we are thinking and choose to become more interested in what we would love—rather than the old automatic patterns of our thinking that give us so many reasons why it's a bad idea to "go for that dream"—only then will we begin to create a physical reality that we love.

We are "thinking" when we are in our creative access; when we are generating in harmony with our own essence, ideas, images, and answers. The nervous system is wired to notify you when you are out of harmony, and when you start to feel contracted, constricted, anxious, worried, or frustrated.

All of those things are reflections of states of mind, where we are looking at a circumstance and viewing it from a certain viewpoint; from a certain frequency. The "trouble at the border" comes when you and I have an image, and we don't know how to traverse the gap between the invisible—what we are imagining—and the physical.

We will develop the steps of getting through the border later on in this book, but for now, and in review, here are the steps we've covered above:

- Create the vision.
- Be "Awake" to the gap of being "at the border."
- Be "Awake" to the automatic voices that will encourage you to stop and turn around.
- Take the action steps in the direction of your vision, despite any lingering doubts.

Our mind is an awesome power, and we are the only species that has been blessed with a mind as powerful as ours. So let's be sure to use it to our advantage and make sure we are, more often than not, choosing the highest and most generative ideas possible.

Again, imagination is very similar to, yet different from, intuition. It's the creativity of what I'm being told through my intuition. Imagination is that creative piece. It's the action step of intuition. It's the actions that are taken *after* you have listened to your intuition.

The Two Sides of Imagination

At least when you are in a state of being "Awake," it becomes this creative tool; when I use my imagination correctly, that is. This is because we can use our mind to come up with all sorts of imaginative things—both things that would forward our vision, or thwart our vision. But it's important to check in to see how we are using this faculty. Are these creations going to enhance our lives, or be fuel for a fire of destruction?

Our minds are quite capable of using imaginative thoughts that are not derived from intuition, but rather birthed from a place of fear. That is why it is so important to be "Awake" and to remain awake while we use this powerful tool called imagination.

In other words, unless we are careful, imagination has the potential to destroy and tear things apart. It can take us down a path that is neither empowered nor positive in growth. That is because it is fear-based. It is using the power of our minds, driven by our deepest fears, to fuel our subconscious operating system.

This brings us right back to the circle of intuition and imagination. It takes us to that place where we listen to the intuition and use the ideas that come to us for empowerment, or even protection, and use these ideas to take action to enhance our lives.

When it's used properly in a positive and proactive way, the tag-team of intuition and imagination can be a powerful one-two punch indeed. Likewise, it can show up in our life as a powerful one-two punch in a not so nice way—if what is driving it is in fact fear-based thinking.

What if My Imagination Only Creates Chaos and Fear?

There is a duality to imagination in that it can be used either for positive things, or be used to create the negative outcomes you do not wish to experience. But don't be fooled by thinking, "Oh, no. I'd never use my imagination to create the chaos that seems to follow me around like a lost cat looking for a meal!" Of course, we'd never do that, right?

How Can I Think in a New Way that is More of a Positive Tool?

So again, there is duality at play in our lives. Your imagination can be used for very positive and creative ways, or it can be creatively destructive. And this leads us directly to "perception," which will be covered next. Perception, of course, is how we perceive a situation. So something may appear scary, but if you flip it, it's quite possibly the best thing for you, in order to move through a lesson, or what have you.

Turn Up the Volume

Creating an Expansive Life

"Imagination is the most marvelous, miraculous, powerful force the world has ever known."

– Napoleon Hill

What we're going to explore next is how the authority of our thoughts is responsible for creating anything and everything that shows up in our life. This does not mean that "bad" things don't happen, or if they do, that it's our fault. Loved ones die, people get sick or hurt, fighting happens, but our response to these circumstances or conditions determine who **we** will be in what happens next and what actions we will take (or do not take). But what we will begin to look at is how to consciously create a vision-based life, instead of a condition-based existence.

We are going to look at this deeper in Chapter 3, but for now just know that a condition-based existence means we commit only to things we *think* we can achieve. It's about never really testing our greatness, and also how we don't do certain things because we can't see how it's all going to work out. It's the false belief that we don't already have the conditions present that will generate its possibility.

But the good news is, we do have control over our thoughts. And actually, it's the only thing we really do have any control over; our thoughts—and specifically, what we think and when we think it. That's all good, but it takes practice to develop that acumen.

Just know you have an infinite resource with your mind—as long as you are also being "Aware" of these inspiring thoughts coming your way. I like to say, "A thought channeled specifically is like transforming incandescent lighting into a laser."

Reactive States VS. Creative States

By now, we are seeing how being "Awake" is a foundational piece to the big picture. But do you also realize that we need to be awake in order to be aware of this? If you are not awake, and you do not consciously chose your thoughts carefully to craft the life you want to be living—well then, you're pretty much sleepwalking through life.

I don't know what the percentage of the planet is in a state of sleepwalking, but I suspect it is very, very high. A great example of this is the movie *I Am Legend* starring Will Smith. In that film, the people who have "been infected" have to hide in the dark and can't come out into the light. They are completely in a reactive state of mind; they are in survival mode. They simply exist. Will Smith's character dreams of a way to lift their maladies, but they can't even hear him; they simply want to kill him because he isn't like them. It's such a powerful movie, when you dive deep into the core metaphors presented. Sounds like the world, doesn't it?

If we could only wake up to being supported in life—to look newly to distinguish our thinking, to learn that what we control *is* our thinking—we'd find that that is more than enough to create the life we would love living. And, that there is support for all of us.

You see, a reactive life is not at all a creative life. No, let me correct that statement. It is creative, but what exactly are you creating? An uplifting movie such as *It's a Wonderful Life* or a horror movie like *I Am Legend* essentially reveals that.

How Do I Hear the Good Amidst All the Other Noise in My Head?

Based on your thoughts and actions, are you creating an expansive creative life? Or are you constantly reacting to your circumstances and creating a life by default? You know, that same day over and over again, different occurrences, but essentially the same life. It's really not that hard to identify. Would you define your current life as expansive and growing? Or perhaps is it restrictive and sucking the vitality right out of you. And it doesn't even have to be that everything is one way or another. You may have certain areas of your life that are on fire in a good way, but there are other areas that are certainly quite restrictive and have you in a stranglehold.

If I Get My Hopes Too High, Won't the Fall Be That Much Harder?

The key is to strive to have expansive creativity in all areas of your life, and not just some. What works in your personal relationships can also certainly work for and in terms of your finances. As such, habits and practices that work well for your health can also work in building your career. It's all universal in nature.

As you "Awaken," practice seeing things good in your life grow. Choose to be proactive rather than reactive, and see how different your results can be.

The Wealth Maven's review:

How does being "Awake" show up in terms of your own paradigm around money? And don't think you don't have one, because everyone does. Some of us may simply have more limiting ones than others, but we all have them at a certain level or another.

Paradigms are basically a patterned way of thinking that runs automatically. We are living our lives, handling money, and navigating relationships either by design or by default. And, if you're not "Awake" to your thinking, or about who is doing the thinking, then you are living a life of default. You are living on remote, what you have known, been taught, found justification for; the same life, day after day after day.

Take inventory to see if you've been in debt because it was familiar, or just because there was "no thinking" around purchasing certain things, since for you it wasn't really an option anyway. See if you get tangled up in obligations, when you didn't know how you were going to pay for it, or justified it. Or, you had a thought, "I don't care about the results, I'm doing it anyway." The "I don't care" is reactive, a default, without thinking of a larger vision. Wake up. Just look at what you're doing—and take a good look at what you're thinking.

Also take a look at what your spending habits are. The bottom line is that making more money does not solve old patterned ways of spending. Plenty of people who "make a lot of money" are still in old spending patterns, just like people who "don't make a lot of money" are in old spending patterns. The key is to first "Awaken" to what you are doing. Then to begin getting curious as to what would be possible; and what you would really, really love.

CHAPTER 3
PERCEPTION

In This Chapter

* Diving into aspects of how we can shape the very fabric of our lives
* Overcoming perceived circumstances and choosing our conditions
* Seeing there is more than meets the eye in most situations

"We must learn to reawaken and keep ourselves awake, not by mechanical aid, but by an infinite expectation of the dawn."

– Henry David Thoreau

Next, we will explore a third mental faculty, which is the gift of perception. And for me, this is the most important subset: since *how* we see a situation is ultimately how we will create its result. Perception has two sides to it, just like imagination. But in this case, perception has another vocabulary word we can grab onto, which is "perspective." And yet, there is a very different energy about the word *perspective* relative to perception.

Perspective is from the world, whereas perception is from our guidance. Which leads us right back to where we began, and that is with the gift of intuition. As you can see, there is a very profound circle of knowledge here in the three elements of intuition, imagination, and perception; each has the great potential to work beautifully with one another and in such a positive and creative way.

To take this a step further, let's look at when someone is asked, "What is your perception?" Their answer is typically from their perspective, from outside sources, conditions, and results—not from their perception. That is coming from your area of judgment. That's coming from your navigating within this world. It is not coming from you, and your inner guidance. Your perception is so much deeper than that, and it is something that you claim. It's how you are able to reframe something.

Per·cep·tion *per-sep-shun* noun

the way you think about or understand someone or something; an ability to understand or notice something easily.

"A writer of considerable perception, she remembers how it feels to be confused and insecure."

synonyms: *discernment, insight, wisdom; perceptiveness*

The way that you notice or understand something using one of your senses.

"a growing perception of the enormity of the problem."

synonyms: *perceptivity, sagaciousness, sagacity, sageness; discernment*

The gifts that lie within our perceptions are critical in choosing a more enlivening way to be in the world. And there is not a moment within our lives when we are not actively using this mental faculty. The key thing to remember here is that its true power lies in the way we use it—every day and in every way. But know this, the subtlety and simplicity of how we are able to shift our perceptions is deceptive. So don't let this fool you into believing it is not important.

Perception has the power to transform even the most difficult and overwhelming challenges into minor setbacks, or in fact make them disappear altogether. It can also be the thing that surrounds you with new opportunities and possibilities, and what catapults your life into an entirely new world.

Perceived Point of View

Perception is knowing that I am the one who gets to choose what any situation means to me. I get to make the final decision about what this or that means. And, to me, perception is empowering. Always.

On the other hand, "perspective" is more often on the side of disempowerment. It's typically fearful. It's a "watch your back" kind of energy; reading into the situation what is wrong. Perception doesn't have what is wrong; it has a way of seeing the possibility in all situations.

When on the surface it appears either right or wrong, perception puts the power back in me. The true strength here is that I get to choose and control my thoughts, and be awake to this fact. This is an awakened thought, the notion that you get to choose.

Many people are running around thinking that life is happening to them. But in fact, life is happening *through* them. You have a choice as to what thoughts you will entertain. What thoughts you will focus your energy upon. And in fact, those thoughts you do choose will shape the very fabric of your life. Being "Awake" to that is both profound and potentially life changing.

Conditions & Circumstances

Infinite Possibilities

"If the doors of perception were cleansed, everything would appear to man as it is, infinite."

– William Blake

Someone once said, "We are just a panel of buttons with responses programmed in, and when something triggers one of these buttons, we are simply given the response that had been programmed into that button." We emotionalize the content with our opinions or judgments. We live with conditions, circumstances, and what I will call "the content" of our life. We gain clarity of life (and peace of mind) when we accept the content—not condone it, but accept it, exactly as it is.

Alternately, if we resist it, we set up a rigid vibration in our own bodies and minds, from which little advancement or creative solution can result. We tend to emotionalize the content with our opinions, judgments, and our own story; whether it looks like a problem or it looks like a blessing.

Just for now, look at the emotional charge you have on anything that's happening in your life at present. Whether you're getting married, or you're getting divorced; whether there is somebody coming into your life, or somebody is leaving; whether there is money in the bank, or it looks like scarcity, realize that no matter what the content is, or what is happening, ultimately it's neutral—and it remains that way until we "charge" it with an opinion. In other words, what are YOU saying about it to yourself?

What is happening doesn't have a charge on it until we give it one, with the meaning we impose on it. It has come to bless us, if we can see the gift that it brings. That may sound insane, but when I choose my perception as "there's good that will come out of this situation, condition, and/or relationship" I will act and respond and become "Awake" to what can be revealed for my good (and the good of others).

This is what I am asking you to do, or at least begin to be "Awake" to its possibility and potential. Take a look at your conditions and situations from an inner knowing, an inner perception; and not just from the perspective of the world, of judgments, and of right or wrong. Become "Awake" to what every situation can provide as a gift to you.

Our focus, therefore, should be on how to utilize the daily content of our lives to help us move directly, distinctly, and powerfully toward the intentions we have in our heart and awakened mind. The next part of our work is looking for the direction of the life we would love living, and consciously designing and selecting action steps to take us "across the border" into the physical reality of that imagined life.

Tapping Into the Possibilities

When I look for what is working, what is harmonious with being "Awake" to a life—a world which is empowering, providing opportunities for growth and personal evolution, even though the situation may not be what I prefer it to look like—I can still look for, and be "Awake" to, an opportunity, a blessing in the situation. It's a matter of reprogramming "how I look at something."

That is where the expansive and unlimited possibilities lie. Going with the flow of our natural currents in life is where the magic is. You actually would have to force something limiting into existence. What is natural is what's expansive in our lives; what is good, loving, and abundant. It takes much more energy to keep what you would really love away from you than to allow and "make welcome" what is abundant, that which is seeking you.

What's a whole lot easier is to release any resistance to what's happening and be "Awake" to your life, the conditions, and also the desires. Begin to observe that, and be "Awake" to life. When we release resistance of the current conditions, it becomes so much easier to be surrounded by the good that is already there. So stop seeing "what's wrong" and interpreting conditions or circumstance from your past experiences as bad. Get more interested in what's possible, and in what you would love. Don't deny or ignore the circumstances or conditions. Simply deny their power over you.

Blessings in Disguise

Just know the content of our life has come to bless us; my dear friend and mentor, Mary Morrissey, taught me that from the beginning of our relationship. Life has come to bless us. It is simply our choice as to how we will perceive it as such. Really, there is nothing that doesn't contain a blessing, if we are willing to see life as that. What we are doing is training ourselves to leave conditioned-based thinking (what we see showing up in our conditions and our circumstances as the *truth* about our life) behind, to create a vision-based (what we would love) life going forward.

Our current results, and our current conditions, come from the brain's patterned synaptic pathways of our past thinking. Much like a computer's operating system, our subconscious runs off of a program. And what we're doing here, by using intentions that are independent of conditions, is installing a new operating system, in order to have new programming that create better results.

Here is an example to both of the points above:

Oh, the work to be done in releasing our "selves" into the flow of good. It can be such a journey at times. But always remember, it is not natural to maintain something limiting in our lives. What is natural is to be free flowing and effortless.

Nothing But the "Truth" – No Facts Allowed

So let's move on to distinguish the difference between facts and truth. A fact is what is the manifested condition currently, or the manifested condition of our past. Those are facts—what has manifested in the condition of three-dimensional "reality, time, and space."

In my example above, fact—I was divorced for the second time; fact—my son was moving to live with his dad; fact—I had just turned forty years old.

But here's what is so: facts don't determine your future. So let's say you're committed to the idea that "I will never be able to..." do, or have, something in particular, because of some past fact (and be assured, you have very good reasons and evidence why that's true). This could be either something I did or didn't do, something that was done to me, or something like, "I never went to college, so I am going to forever be..." That's a *story* about facts. It's not the truth.

We are only limited by our own thoughts and what we make our conditions mean—about us, other people, the situation, about life. We are never defined by our past unless we say so; we are not limited by the conditions of our upbringing, unless we make an agreement with that.

So again, you don't deny the facts, just as you don't deny the conditions. But you certainly deny their power to define you and your future. You are not defined by your history. You are not defined by your conditions. So this is where we work with our thinking and our perspective, *or* our perception.

What is true is that life shows up consistent with what you are committed to. So, you and I practice getting committed to being in harmony in our thinking—with what we would love to have, do, and be—regardless of the conditions. A great example for me when I was an investment advisor was in attending the Barron's "Top Women Advisors" meeting for the first time in 2008. Facts may have said this was impossible, but the truth was it became my reality.

I was thrilled and excited to be asked and to attend. I noticed when I was getting ready for the first evening dinner and presentation that I was worried about what I brought to wear, how tired I thought that I looked, and what I would say to the other top advisors. I felt like a fraud, a misplaced wannabe, and a phony. These were all from a limiting perception from my own programming.

I reached out to my mentor for coaching to be "re-minded" (I love that word; to be "minded-again"; to think newly) that these were only thoughts from a limited opinion of myself; and that there is a truth greater than identifying with my condition based, little self, who compared herself with others and hence, immediately became "not enough." I simply had to reprogram by reminding myself that I had been invited, and was committed to contributing a thought, an idea, a way of doing business, that could make a difference for someone, and committed to making a new friend. Basically, some *other* thought about why I accepted the invitation, rather than the thoughts of "you're not qualified to be here."

Greater Than Any Conditions or Circumstance

If conditions are challenging (time restraints, traffic, something to get handled that wasn't anticipated, child gets sick or hurt, business deal fell through, spouse gets laid off, the economy is terrible, and on and on...) what do you make these conditions and circumstances mean? Is "it" awful? This shouldn't be that way? There must be something wrong with me?

If you remember anything from this material, remember this: HOW we look at something (is it good/bad, this should or shouldn't be happening, is it just not right or is it wrong?), including my relationship with it (am I in the "can/can't" state of mind), is simply just a thought—a powerful thought! And it will determine your next action step and your *next* thought. The best news? *You* have authority over what you will think—

that is, *if* you are "Awake"! And the potential in all of us is always greater than any circumstance or condition.

Say you want a particular house that overlooks the ocean, or the forest, or the mountains, but you only have a certain amount of money available for the purchase. Again, that's a fact, but the *truth* is that we are unlimited beings. Much of this series on "Real Wealth" is to begin to experience this knowing from deep inside of us.

As you begin this journey in thinking newly, in being "Awake" to your thoughts, you begin to pattern a life in harmony. Who is this woman/man that is living in that house? What is she like? What does she think about? Who are her friends? What does she put her time and energy into? You begin to be the person who lives the life you are imagining.

Now this is all a practice and that's a good thing. And you don't have to take it on all at once. Just a little at a time, and you can do this a little bit each day. Start noticing when you begin to feel constricted. You are paddling upstream. Are you are feeling in a flow with ease and grace? Then you are in the current of your own life. When you start to feel constricted, notice that you've got some story going on about a condition.

In that moment differentiate between the condition, which is a fact, but perhaps there is a truth that is underneath, around, on top of, or infused into this circumstance that is bigger than the circumstance itself. In fact, you are way bigger than any such circumstance that leaves you feeling constricted. What I am thinking *about* the condition or myself is actually what is limiting me.

Again, just remember, this is a practice...so just play with it and have fun along the way!!!

We are so sensitive today, because there are so many things to be sensitive about. Things are coming at us so fast, and there is so much more information coming at us than ever before. There is so much to deal with; so much more than ever before. Our parents didn't deal with anything that we are dealing with. We experience in a single day what some people never experience over entire lifetimes—there are so many choices, decisions, and interactions now than there were even fifty years ago.

Seriously, How Can I Navigate Through This Mess?

Doing so may be courageous, but believe me, you are up for the task once you are awake and aware. It is almost as if it becomes second nature to stand firmly in "who I am" no matter what is happening around me.

Understanding There Is More

Eternal Freedoms of Choice

"It exists within and around us at all time, we simply have to expand our awareness to be able to perceive it."

– Laurel Geise, author of The Jesus Seeds

The above quote from author Laurel Geise is in reference to an expanded awareness. You see, we intuitively know we have this ability that guides us along the path of remembering, by using intuition to navigate the evolutionary pathway to the remembrance of your magnificence. This is one way in particular that we're able to understand there is more.

In terms of perception, we can land squarely in the debate about good or bad, right or wrong. And there are great cases for both sides of the argument. How can it be true that "nothing is bad unless you think it's bad," is a statement I have frequently heard over the years. My first response is, that's not true, and there are bad things in this world. What about murder, war, car wrecks, and things like that?

The Gift of Time in Collecting One's Thoughts

Even so, I have come to learn that there is more to this than first meets the eye. The next time something that you are tempted to say is bad, hold off and instead—as my mentor always says—hit your internal pause button to wait a few days. Just like the age-old suggestion for times when you receive a nasty letter, or other form of communication. Wait at least twenty-four hours before you reply.

Good advice. Take at least twenty-four hours to cool off before sending back an email or text reply, or picking up the phone to respond. Sure, you may write out what you think you want to say in reply, but after twenty-four hours, you'll likely have a slightly different thought about it—that is if you're willing to come from your gift of perception (an inside/out reality) rather than perspective (an outside/in reality)—and would rather soften up the tone in response.

The bottom line is to give yourself the gift of time to collect your thoughts and to see what gifts actually may be hidden just under the surface. Be sure to use this gift of perception often.

Stop.
Take a Deep Breath.
Look at and Get Curious About
   1) what is seeking to emerge
   2) what is wanting to be revealed
   3) what is my underlying commitment

Time and time again, I have heard remarkable stories from friends, where after seeing a situation in hindsight, and after the elapse of time, they realized the original upset actually became a blessing in disguise.

Stories where a husband gets laid off from work, and at first there is panic over how they would be able to pay the monthly bills, but after a very short time a new and better job shows up. Or when a boyfriend or lover breaks it off, and you think the world has literally ended, only to meet the "love of your life" within a few short months. This happens over and over again— and I personally know of dozens of stories just like the ones mentioned above.

So keep an open mind when it comes to judging whether something is good or bad. Look for the blessings in everything, and I mean everything. If you do, you will undoubtedly find them.

Even so, the best lesson you will find in this practice is that you can *choose* how you are going to feel about something.

Even in the presence of a circumstance that is certainly not something you'd prefer to have, you can make a choice to not suffer with it, as you may have done in the past. You can choose how you respond, rather than react.

The good news is that we have access to our internal programming, and we can upgrade it at any time. It is for us to learn, grow, and expand into better and better versions of ourselves. Hopefully, none of us will ever have to face such horrible circumstances as Viktor Frankl did, but know this—if we had to, we too could steer our thoughts and actions toward a higher purpose, and experience the beauty that can follow.

Our Perceptions Create Our Realities

Another way to illustrate this point is with something Bob Proctor once said (and I love his explanation) which was, "The answer to any challenge that comes to us is already here; it's our perception that tells us we cannot solve the problem. Perceptions are our reality. Our perception creates our reality. It's how we see the situation."

He goes on to say, "What we have to understand is that our perceptions are formed by our paradigm. Our paradigm is nothing but a multitude of ideas that are fixed in our subconscious mind, and it's the paradigm that causes us to look at things the way we're looking at them. You may take your income and ask yourself how could I multiply it. How could I turn my annual income to a monthly income?" Now, from your point of view, from where you are right now, you may instantly say, "I'd never be able to do that," and you're right, *from your point of view.*

Bob continues with, "But if you had somebody else's point of view, somebody that was earning that much money, they could probably sit down and they might say, "Well I could show you a number of different ways to do this," and that's because they're looking at it from another place." I would actually change Bob's word *perception* to *perspective*, as the "somebody else's point of view" is what actually shifts the demeaning perspective into the perceptive possibility.

We'll get into how paradigms really work later on in Chapter 5, (In the next part of the series, AWARE) as we dive deeper into our thinking patterns and the "glass ceilings" each and every one of us has.

Is There More at Play Here Than Meets the Eye?

We must always remember to have a more elevated view within our lives. If we go through life looking at it from a ground-level perspective, then we miss out on the 30,000-foot view, or the infinite view of what's really going on. We can rise above the problems and circumstances of our daily lives and see more.

Does Perception Have Two Sides Similar to Imagination?

The trick is to change our perceptions of situations and realize that they are neither bad nor good—they are just what is, and we can make of it what we want to make of it. As James Allen said, "Uncrown the circumstance and let it fill its servant's place." So that is what we must do—open up to our perceptions when necessary to lead a larger and more expansive life, rather than stay in the outside-in world of perspective.

The Wealth Maven's Review:

Ask yourself several times during the day, "What am I awake to in this room, this building, this situation?" Look around and be "Awake" to physical objects and other people. Bring consciousness to the moment. Be present. This is what it is to being awake—"Awake" to the fact that everything is in relationship to, and with, everything else.

Again, everything is in relationship to everything else. For example, I am in relationship with the chair I sit in. I am in relationship, not only with others, but with everything else. I have a relationship with the weather, with the dog, with the paintings on the wall. How I interact with any of them typically determines how I interact with all of them. Am I casual in my relationship with my own body? Am I casual in my relationship with another human being? Am I vibrant in being "Awake" to my ability to think, to interact with the physical world and ultimately with Life itself?

Here is an interesting tidbit I once heard someone share. When asked how he was doing, his reply was, "I'm doing great; just grateful that I got to wake up this morning instead of coming to." The profound wisdom of that comment is that he was being "Awake." Awakened in life, for the mere pleasure, the mere gift of Life itself. He was being "Awake" to the new day and what could be revealed beautifully and naturally in that day; rather than having to be hurt, or feel the pain of not being "Awake," or as he so eloquently put it, "coming to."

AFTERWORD
REAL WEALTH

In Closing...

* Proceeding from "Awake" to the principle of "Aware"
* Areas of support that are available
* Other programs, services, and presentations that are offered

"Only by awakening can you know the true meaning of that word. A glimpse is enough to initiate the awakening process, which is irreversible."

– Eckhart Tolle

At this point, you are getting an idea of what "Real Wealth" truly is. You have now just completed the first of four pillars that make up the full-spectrum "Real Wealth" system. This is a system that can bring you in alignment with having not only material wealth, but elevated results in all of the other areas of your life. Once you are versed in being fully "Awake" to all that you do—and in how you are "being" on a day-to-day basis— you are ready for the next of four cornerstones, which is the pillar of being "Aware."

Remember, this is a system that builds one upon another, and a method that has proven to be very effective in retraining your brain so it can support you in achieving all of your dreams. By moving from "Awake" to the principle of "Aware," you will be progressing in the right direction.

From Awake to Aware...

Real Wealth Revealed: The Secret Logic of Becoming Rich is a 4-part series of books that covers the cornerstones, or pillars of foundation, that support a full-spectrum life. Now that we are "Awake" to how creative our thoughts are, and that our thoughts are what we can control,, we have jumped head-first into areas of our thinking, and have seen just how powerful our mind can be used as a tool, we next move on to the area of being "Aware." This is where we take a look at our behaviors and the patterns that are running our lives. We begin to deeply notice what we are noticing, and begin to transform the way we behave and show up as human beings.

Going Beyond Success

A 4-Step Guide to Living a Life You Love

"The future belongs to those who believe in the beauty of their dreams."

– Eleanor Roosevelt

I am a certified coach—and a results expert. As the founder of the Going Beyond Success" full-spectrum personal development training system, I can assist you in designing a vision for a harmonious life with equity given to all facets and then provide the tools to navigate the gap between the life that you are living now and the life that you are imagining.

How I Can help...

I teach cutting-edge technology—a technology of thinking—a way of thinking that improves and alters goal achievement with ease and creativity, and is designed to eliminate competition.

Everything is energy. Everything is a vibration. You experience it personally even in your own body. You feel it when you walk into a room—that is, if you're awake. This is a technology of thinking, and of how you think to redesign the patterns programmed from the past. I teach the structure of creating results, in lieu of doing the activities that force the results.

In other words, I teach a structure for awareness of what you really are thinking, and the thinking that is creating your current results.

Once that is addressed, we then design the structure that will develop the results that you would love to have. Ideas come to you in an instant—in a state of vision. This is part of the technology that I teach. The first thing we create is a vision in all four major areas of your life: health, wealth, career, and relationships.

Why I work with successful women in particular is because they have an instinct—an intuitive knowing of how to be, and how to create a business by taking care of their clients in a profound way. These women are also receiving value for the value they provide—it's a perfect circle, a cycle of creativity.

But, oftentimes, that "knowing" doesn't translate to other areas of their life. I provide the support to decode what has been working and translate it to the other areas in life that you, personally, would love to have developed and translated into a full-spectrum life. It matters what we think and how we think about "it"; in other words, what our thinking *is* about.

I also coach on the development of character, in a way that magnifies the overall development of the psyche and worldly achievements. As noted, this is coaching for a full-spectrum life that goes beyond success.

ABOUT THE AUTHOR...

As CEO of MMC&C, Marilyn J. Macha is a well-known business owner and investment advisor to high net worth individuals and families, whose primary goal has been to address important issues she observed in her career as a wealth advisor. In her latest book, *Real Wealth Revealed: The Secret Logic of Becoming Rich*, focuses on just that. The crux of the book's message is to illuminate the reader to the fact that creating real financial wealth requires the simultaneous creation of a successful and balanced personal life. One is required to support the other in order to create real and authentic financial success and a wealthy life.

Ms. Macha has also commenced the writing of two new books. *Designing Business with Heart* is a story that relates to operating a successful business and maintaining a heartfelt attitude with clients, associates, and employees. *Women Influencing Business* examines the role of high-profile women operating successful businesses and how they influence the corporate culture of their organizations.

Keynote Speeches and Presentations

Ms. Macha has developed a series of keynote speeches designed for corporate meetings and retreats; it is also possible for her to design custom presentations for special company events (e.g., business anniversary key accomplishments, etc.).

The standard keynote presentations relate to the following topics:

- Women's Leadership
- Women Finding Balance in a Man's World
- Creating Real Wealth
- Claiming Your Vision

4-Month Study Programs

The Company also provides a live and recorded four month study course using video technology and are taught by Ms. Macha. They include a 60-minute weekly live teaching presentation supported by a workbook and/or other course materials. There is a Q&A session provided for each course and all programs are recorded for use by members who may miss a program or who wish to re-audit.

Organizational Consulting and Coaching

The Company provides business clients organizational consulting on a defined scope of services designed for a variety of situations; e.g., leadership changes, M&A activities, strategic planning, customer loyalty, and customer service. It also supports transformational consulting working with groups and teams within organizations to support for higher productivity and profitability.

Executive Coaching

Ms. Macha can be retained for 6-month or 12-month Executive Coaching engagements. These engagements are typically with C-level management as well as divisional leadership focused on leadership and personal excellence, and peak performance.

For more information or to engage Marilyn for an event please inquire at Marilyn@marilynmacha.com

For Free resources and information visit www.MarilynMacha.com

NOTES

I've added some NOTES pages where you can quickly jot down any thought, idea or inspiration which comes to you while reading the book.

_____

_____

_____

_____

_____

_____

_____

_____

_____

_____

NOTES

_____

_____

_____

_____

_____

_____

_____

_____

_____

_____

_____

NOTES

_____

_____

_____

_____

_____

_____

_____

_____

_____

_____

_____

NOTES

_____

_____

_____

_____

_____

_____

_____

_____

_____

_____

_____

NOTES

_____

_____

_____

_____

_____

_____

_____

_____

_____

_____

_____

NOTES

_____

_____

_____

_____

_____

_____

_____

_____

_____

_____

_____

NOTES

NOTES

_____

_____

_____

_____

_____

_____

_____

_____

_____

_____

_____

_____

NOTES

_____

_____

_____

_____

_____

_____

_____

_____

_____

_____

_____

NOTES

_____

_____

_____

_____

_____

_____

_____

_____

_____

_____

_____

NOTES

NOTES

_____

_____

_____

_____

_____

_____

_____

_____

_____

_____

_____

_____

NOTES

_____

_____

_____

_____

_____

_____

_____

_____

_____

_____

_____

NOTES

_____

_____

_____

_____

_____

_____

_____

_____

_____

_____

_____

NOTES

NOTES

NOTES